Boring Rick and the Junk Factory Mystery

PHASE 5

/y/

Level 8 – Purple

Helpful Hints for Reading at Home

The graphemes (written letters) and phonemes (units of sound) used throughout this series are aligned with Letters and Sounds. This offers a consistent approach to learning whether reading at home or in the classroom.

HERE IS A LIST OF PHONEMES FOR THIS PHASE OF LEARNING. AN EXAMPLE OF THE PRONUNCIATION CAN BE FOUND IN BRACKETS.

Phase 5			
ay (day)	ou (out)	ie (tie)	ea (eat)
oy (boy)	ir (girl)	ue (blue)	aw (saw)
wh (when)	ph (photo)	ew (new)	oe (toe)
au (Paul)	a_e (make)	e_e (these)	i_e (like)
o_e (home)	u_e (rule)		

Phase 5 Alternative Pronunciations of Graphemes			
a (hat, what)	e (bed, she)	i (fin, find)	o (hot, so, other)
u (but, unit)	c (cat, cent)	g (got, giant)	ow (cow, blow)
ie (tied, field)	ea (eat, bread)	er (farmer, herb)	ch (chin, school, chef)
y (yes, by, very)	ou (out, shoulder, could, you)		

HERE ARE SOME WORDS WHICH YOUR CHILD MAY FIND TRICKY.

Phase 5 Tricky Words			
oh	their	people	Mr
Mrs	looked	called	asked
could			

TOP TIPS FOR HELPING YOUR CHILD TO READ:

- Allow children time to break down unfamiliar words into units of sound and then encourage children to string these sounds together to create the word.

- Encourage your child to point out any focus phonics when they are used.

- Read through the book more than once to grow confidence.

- Ask simple questions about the text to assess understanding.

- Encourage children to use illustrations as prompts.

PHASE 5
/y/

This book focuses on the grapheme /y/ and is a purple level 8 book band.

Boring Rick and the Junk Factory Mystery

Written by
William Anthony

Illustrated by
Kris Jones

Boring Rick put the plastic in the left bin.
Boring Rick put the metal in the right bin.
Boring Rick's day was done at the junk factory and he went home in his boring car.

Boring Rick had a boring life. He did not ask about anything. He did not moan about anything. He barely said anything at all.

Boring Rick's son, Bryn, was not as boring as his dad. Bryn did ask about things. One day he asked, "where does the junk go after you sort it into bins at the junk factory?"

"We just recycle it, Bryn," said Boring Rick in his typical boring tone.
But then a spark flashed in his mind.
The spark jumped from his mind and turned into a butterfly in his tummy.

Was Boring Rick really sure that was what happened to the junk? After all, his boss had always been very shady about how the factory's system worked.

Boring Rick was not sure at all. In fact, he needed to find out. For the very first time in his life, Boring Rick felt a bit less boring.

The next day, Less Boring Rick plodded into work. He put the plastic in the left bin. He put the metal in the right bin. Then, Less Boring Rick checked to see if anyone was watching.

The coast was clear. He followed the plastic bin pipe. He followed it off the factory floor, down the stairs and round the bend, all the way to a hole in a wall.

Less Boring Rick bent down and put his eye to a gap between the pipe and the wall.

Lorries. Lots of lorries. Each lorry was collecting plastic or metal and whizzing off.

Every lorry had a logo that read 'Pranton in the Sky'. This was all very odd.
Less Boring Rick picked up a nearby chopper and swung. That was pretty reckless, even for Less Boring Rick.

Reckless Rick smashed the wall and sneaked toward a lorry in the loading bay. He was lucky no one saw him being so reckless. "Pranton in the Sky, what is that all about?" he muttered.

The plastic pipe filled the lorry. Feeling more reckless than ever, Reckless Rick grabbed onto the back. He hoped the lorry might carry him to where he could work out the mystery!

The lorry whisked Reckless Rick out of a tunnel, into a forest, over a mountain and into a field. He had no idea what this place was for, but it was really far from home.

The field was empty, apart from the lorry full of plastic, Reckless Rick and a gigantic conveyor belt that reached up into the clouds. It went so high that Reckless Rick could not see the end.

It was a shame that Reckless Rick did not have time to think. Without warning, the lorry tipped back and dropped all the plastic – and Reckless Rick – onto the conveyor belt.

By the time Reckless Rick had pulled himself out of the plastic pile, he was as high as the clouds. This was not good. In fact, it was bad. Very bad.

The conveyor belt pushed past the clouds and kept going. It went past the Moon and beyond the stars.

Things had gone from very bad to totally awful. Reckless Rick never intended to go intergalactic.

Intergalactic Rick looked up. The conveyor belt seemed to finally have an end. It stopped at a small, pink planet with a big flag sticking out of it…
'PRANTON'!

The conveyor belt dumped Intergalactic Rick on the dusty ground, under the pile of plastic. "So Pranton in the Sky is a planet?" he gasped. Intergalactic Rick really did not mean to end up here.

The odd people on Pranton were melting down all the plastic and metal from the junk factory back on Earth.

"But why?" wondered Intergalactic Rick. "What do they need it all for?"

The Pranton people were tipping the melted plastic and metal into machines that seemed to be printing objects. Every time they printed an object, they all shouted "PRANTON!" in a short, sharp burst.

Intergalactic Rick was trying to work out whether the Pranton people were just saying the word 'printing' wrong, when he made a sound he did not mean to make. A toot from Intergalactic Rick's bottom alerted them.

They gathered around him. Sadly for Intergalactic Rick, they did not look happy. He was totally busted.
Busted Rick only had one choice left.
He got out his phone and called the Queen back on Earth.

The Queen was not pleased with the news. "They are stealing our junk? Don't worry, I will fire the missiles!" she yelled.
"No!" panicked Busted Rick. "I am ON the pla–"

But it was too late. Busted Rick could see the missiles coming past the Moon and the stars. Silly Busted Rick. He could have just sorted the plastic and the metal and been boring. Instead, he somehow started an intergalactic war.

Oh dear, Lonely Rick.

Boring Rick and the Junk Factory Mystery

1) Which of these versions of Rick comes last in the story?
   a) Lonely Rick
   b) Intergalactic Rick
   c) Busted Rick

2) What is Pranton in the Sky?

3) What does Rick find in a big empty field?

4) What is a mystery?

5) Do you think it is better to solve a mystery or to leave it alone?

BookLife
PUBLISHING

BookLife Readers

© 2022 **BookLife Publishing Ltd.**
King's Lynn, Norfolk, PE30 4LS, UK

ISBN 978-1-80155-528-9

All rights reserved. Printed in Poland.
A catalogue record for this book is available from the British Library.

Boring Rick and the Junk Factory
Written by William Anthony
Illustrated by Kris Jones

An Introduction to BookLife Readers...

Our Readers have been specifically created in line with the London Institute of Education's approach to book banding and are phonetically decodable and ordered to support each phase of the Letters and Sounds document.

Each book has been created to provide the best possible reading and learning experience. Our aim is to share our love of books with children, providing both emerging readers and prolific page-turners with beautiful books that are guaranteed to provoke interest and learning, regardless of ability.

BOOK BAND GRADED using the Institute of Education's approach to levelling.

PHONETICALLY DECODABLE supporting each phase of Letters and Sounds.

EXERCISES AND QUESTIONS to offer reinforcement and to ascertain comprehension.

BEAUTIFULLY ILLUSTRATED to inspire and provoke engagement, providing a variety of styles for the reader to enjoy whilst reading through the series.

AUTHOR INSIGHT:
WILLIAM ANTHONY

William Anthony's involvement with children's education is quite extensive. He has written a vast array of titles for BookLife Publishing, across a wide range of subjects. William graduated from Cardiff University with a 1st Class BA (Hons) in Journalism, Media and Culture, creating an app and a TV series, among other things, during his time there.

William Anthony has also produced work for the Prince's Trust, a charity created by HRH The Prince of Wales, that helps young people with their professional future. He has created animated videos for a children's education company that works closely with the charity.

PHASE 5 /y/

This book focuses on the grapheme /y/ and is a purple level 8 book band.